DOLPHINS SET II

GANGES RIVER DOLPHINS

Kristin Petrie

ABDO Publishing Company

visit us at
www.abdopub.com

Published by ABDO Publishing Company, 4940 Viking Drive, Edina, Minnesota 55435.
Copyright © 2006 by Abdo Consulting Group, Inc. International copyrights reserved in all
countries. No part of this book may be reproduced in any form without written permission from
the publisher. The Checkerboard Library™ is a trademark and logo of ABDO Publishing
Company.

Printed in the United States.

Cover Photo: Peter Arnold
Interior Photos: Corbis pp. 13, 15, 17, 21; © Doug Perrine / SeaPics.com p. 10; Peter Arnold
    p. 19; © Roland Seitre / SeaPics.com p. 5; Uko Gorter pp. 6-7

Series Coordinator: Megan M. Gunderson
Editors: Heidi M. Dahmes, Megan M. Gunderson
Art Direction, Diagram, & Map: Neil Klinepier

Library of Congress Cataloging-in-Publication Data

Petrie, Kristin, 1970-
    Ganges river dolphins / Kristin Petrie.
        p. cm. -- (Dolphins. Set II)
    Includes index.
    ISBN 1-59679-302-3
    1. Ganges dolphin--Juvenile literature. I. Title.

    QL737.C436P483 2005
    599.53'8--dc22
                                                            2005045796

CONTENTS

GANGES RIVER DOLPHINS

Like humans, dolphins are mammals. This means they are warm-blooded, have hair, and nurse their young. Most dolphins live in the ocean. However, some dolphins live in rivers.

The Ganges River dolphin is one of only four freshwater river dolphins in the world. This dolphin's scientific name is *Platanista gangetica gangetica*. Its common name comes from its home in the Ganges River. Along with the Indus River dolphin, it is part of the **family** Platanistidae.

There are differences between this **cetacean** and its ocean-dwelling cousins. The Ganges River dolphin is less social than other dolphins. Its eyesight is especially poor. And, it sometimes swims on its side. One flipper sticks out of the water while the other trails in the riverbed.

**The Ganges River dolphin's unusual features
have given it several nicknames. These include
the blind dolphin and the side-swimming dolphin.**

5

Size, Shape, and Color

The Ganges River dolphin has a plump body. The female is generally larger than the male. Females grow to just over eight feet (2.5 m) long. Males reach lengths of nearly seven feet (2 m). Ganges River dolphins can weigh up to 200 pounds (90 kg).

A large, paddle-like flipper hangs from each side of a Ganges River dolphin's body. A triangular hump, or ridge,

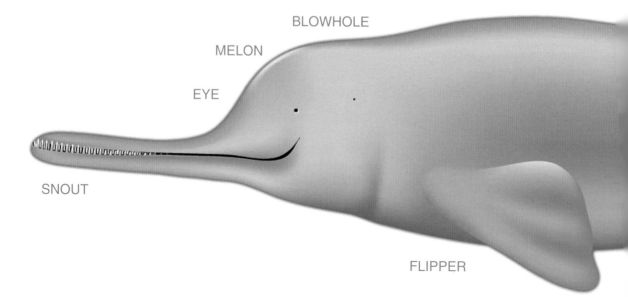

BLOWHOLE

MELON

EYE

SNOUT

FLIPPER

replaces the usual **dorsal** fin. This ridge is one to two inches (3 to 5 cm) high. The dolphin's snout is long and narrow. But, the tip is thicker and sprouts sharp teeth.

Ganges River dolphins have a steep forehead and a rounded **melon**. The blowhole is located above the eye on the left side of the head. They have tiny eyes that cannot see images. Instead, they only use their eyes to detect dark and light.

Ganges River dolphins have solidly gray skin. However, they have also been described as having a blue, gray brown, or chocolate brown color. And, the belly can appear slightly pink.

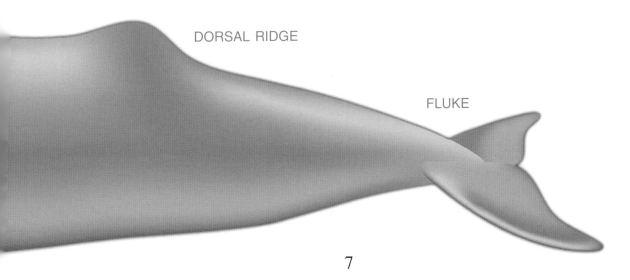

DORSAL RIDGE

FLUKE

WHERE THEY LIVE

The Ganges River dolphin once swam in many Asian rivers. Today, it is found mostly in the rivers of Bangladesh and India. There are also a few in the fast-moving, clear waters of Nepal. Still, the Ganges River dolphin is an **endangered** mammal.

Ganges River dolphins are usually found in areas with slow-moving water. The areas just downstream from where rivers join are also popular spots. They enjoy deep water, but they have been seen in water as shallow as three feet (1 m).

Ganges River dolphins also **migrate** with the seasons. In the dry season, most of the dolphins move to main river channels. In the monsoon, or rainy, season they swim back toward flooded creeks and **tributaries**. Some stay in these river branches during the dry season.

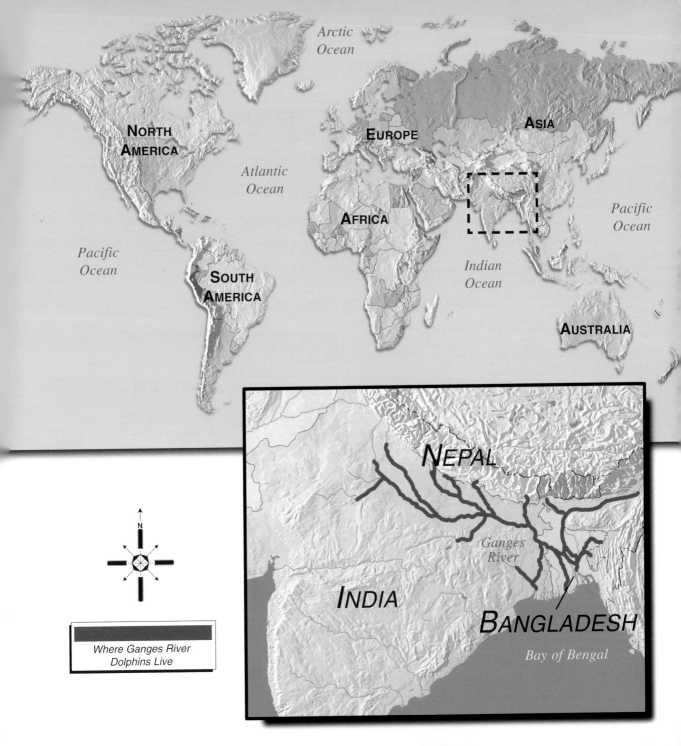

Arctic
Ocean

NORTH
AMERICA

Atlantic
Ocean

EUROPE

ASIA

Pacific
Ocean

Pacific
Ocean

AFRICA

Indian
Ocean

SOUTH
AMERICA

AUSTRALIA

N

Where Ganges River
Dolphins Live

NEPAL

Ganges
River

INDIA

BANGLADESH

Bay of Bengal

SENSES

The Ganges River dolphin's eyes are not helpful in the cloudy Ganges River. So, these dolphins use echolocation to help them survive in their **habitat**. Like a radar system, the dolphin sends noises through the water. These noises echo off objects and return to the dolphin.

Dolphins turn these echoes into information. They can determine where they are and where to go. They can tell the size and shape of the fish around them. In fact, echolocation can even help these talented dolphins tell the difference between similar types of fish!

Atlantic spotted dolphins use echolocation, too. And, they dig in the sand for food.

Dolphins also get information from their sense of touch. This is one of the reasons the Ganges River dolphin swims on its side. In this position, one flipper trails in the water or the mud below. This gives the dolphin information about its surroundings.

Sound wave sent out by dolphin

Echo wave received by dolphin

DEFENSE

It is difficult to know how many Ganges River dolphins remain. This is due in part to their small numbers. And typically, they are seen only when they surface. There may be just a few thousand of these dolphins left. So, they are considered an **endangered** mammal.

With proper attention and **conservation** efforts, this species can still be saved from extinction. But, Ganges River dolphins face several dangers. And, there is little these dolphins can do to defend themselves.

Fishing and pollution are big threats. Large fishing nets can accidentally trap and kill dolphins. And polluted water is bad for the dolphins to swim in. It also kills the fish they feed on.

Opposite page: *The Indus and the Ganges River dolphins are both endangered. This Indus River dolphin has been injured. The World Wide Fund for Nature has a program in Pakistan to help dolphins that have been separated from the rest of their species by dams.*

Another threat to Ganges River dolphins is **habitat** destruction. Dams can separate the dolphins from one another. Dams may also keep dolphins from their feeding grounds. And, they can decrease the number of fish that are available for feeding.

FOOD

The Ganges River dolphin eats a variety of prey. This includes everything from tiny fish to fairly large sharks. The Ganges River dolphin also likes **crustaceans** and squid. When this dolphin is really hungry, even turtles and birds are not safe!

The Ganges River dolphin does much of its feeding on the river floor. Swimming on its side, this dolphin uses one flipper to stir up the mud. This action stirs up food, too.

In deeper areas, the Ganges River dolphin takes short dives to the river bottom. Dives usually last 30 to 90 seconds. But, they can last several minutes. On the river bottom, this dolphin also uses its snout to probe the mud. There, hidden creatures become lunch!

These fishers are drying small fish along the Ganges. When they are eating small fish, Ganges River dolphins may be caught by fishers. Then, the dolphins are sometimes cut up and used as bait for larger fish such as catfish.

BABIES

The Ganges River dolphin is a warm-blooded mammal. Female dolphins are **pregnant** for about 12 months. Then, they typically give birth to one baby.

Baby dolphins are called calves. Ganges River dolphin calves are between 28 and 35 inches (71 and 89 cm) long at birth. Their weight at birth is unknown. But, some scientists estimate that these calves weigh around 17 pounds (8 kg).

Like other mammals, the mother dolphin nurses her baby with milk. Mother and calf stick close together while nursing. A female Ganges River dolphin sometimes carries her calf on her back.

When the calf is one to two months old, it begins to eat prey such as small fish. A calf is **weaned** by one year of age. After the calf is weaned, it goes out on its own.

Many dolphin calves, such as the calf of this bottlenose dolphin, stick close to their mother after birth. This is important while calves are learning to eat and to survive on their own.

BEHAVIORS

Ganges River dolphins usually travel alone or in pairs. Occasionally, they are seen in larger **pods**. They swim constantly. They are usually slow swimmers but can move quickly when needed.

Ganges River dolphins can be seen swimming with their entire snout out of the water. They also show off their short **dorsal** hump when rolling at the surface to breathe.

These dolphins do not usually lift their entire tail out of the water. But when surprised, Ganges River dolphins sometimes **breach**. This activity can give a better view of the species.

Ganges River dolphins also constantly make clicking noises. These noises aid in communication and echolocation. In fact, one of their nicknames is Susu. This name **mimics** the sneezelike sound of the dolphin's breathing.

Most of the time, people can only see a Ganges River dolphin's snout and dorsal hump as it surfaces. When a Ganges River dolphin breaches, people can get a better view of its flukes. But, they will probably still have trouble finding its very small eyes!

GANGES RIVER DOLPHIN FACTS

Scientific Name: *Platanista gangetica gangetica*

Common Names: Susu, Gangetic Dolphin, Blind Dolphin, Side-Swimming Dolphin

Average Size: Females grow to a maximum of just over eight feet (2.5 m) long. Males can grow to nearly seven feet (2 m). Members of this species can weigh up to 200 pounds (90 kg).

Where They're Found: The Ganges River and its branches in India, Bangladesh, and Nepal

Humans affect the Ganges River dolphin's habitat and prey in many ways. They take water for their farms, allow pollution to enter the river, and build dams.

GLOSSARY

breach - to jump or leap up out of the water.

cetacean (sih-TAY-shuhn) - any of various types of mammal, such as the dolphin, that live in water like fish.

conservation - the planned management of natural resources to protect them from damage or destruction.

crustacean (kruhs-TAY-shuhn) - any of a group of animals with hard shells that live mostly in water. Crabs, lobsters, and shrimps are all crustaceans.

dorsal - located near or on the back, especially of an animal.

endangered - in danger of becoming extinct.

family - a group that scientists use to classify similar plants or animals. It ranks above a genus and below an order.

habitat - a place where a living thing is naturally found.

melon - the rounded forehead of some cetaceans, which may aid in echolocation.

migrate - to move from one place to another, often to find food.

mimic - to imitate or copy.

pod - a group of animals, typically whales or dolphins.

pregnant - having one or more babies growing within the body.

tributary - a river or stream that flows into a larger stream, river, or a lake.

wean - to accustom an animal to eat food other than its mother's milk.

WEB SITES

To learn more about Ganges River dolphins, visit ABDO Publishing Company on the World Wide Web at **www.abdopub.com**. Web sites about these dolphins are featured on our Book Links page. These links are routinely monitored and updated to provide the most current information available.

INDEX